The Young Servant's Own Book: Intended As A Present For Girls On First Going Into Service

Samuel Harris And Company

In the interest of creating a more extensive selection of rare historical book reprints, we have chosen to reproduce this title even though it may possibly have occasional imperfections such as missing and blurred pages, missing text, poor pictures, markings, dark backgrounds and other reproduction issues beyond our control. Because this work is culturally important, we have made it available as a part of our commitment to protecting, preserving and promoting the world's literature. Thank you for your understanding.

THE YOUNG SERVANT'S OWN BOOK.

INTENDED AS

A Present for Girls

ON

FIRST GOING INTO SERVICE.

London:
SAML. HARRIS & CO., 5, BISHOPSGATE STREET, E.C.

1883.

Please to read this little book, then put it in your box, and take it out once a year to read over again.

THE YOUNG
SERVANT'S OWN BOOK.

When you think about the time in which you will have to leave home and earn your own bread by service, have you ever considered how happy and comfortable a young servant may feel who loves the Lord Jesus Christ, and is striving to serve her master and mistress faithfully; to do as well when out of their sight as when they are looking at her; who does her own work cheerfully; is ready to help another when needful; who behaves respectfully to her master and mistress; is strictly honest, and very careful to tell the truth?

Now, as I suppose that you will wish to feel happy, whilst gaining an honest and respectable living, I hope some of the following hints may be useful to you.

If you have not a Bible of your own, get one as soon as you are able, that you may read a little in it every day. Look in the New Testament, chiefly, for rules for your conduct; because some things were allowed in former times, and which we read of in the Old Testament, which are not allowed for us to do, being forbidden by our Lord and Saviour to His followers, that is, to Christians.

The Old Testament tells us much of the dealings of God with His chosen people the Jews, and of His will concerning *them*—it also contains many wonderful prophecies respecting our Lord and Saviour Jesus Christ, which were written many hundred years before He came to live on earth.

The New Testament tells us of our Lord and Saviour after He came, and of His will concerning us at the present time.

When you read in the Bible, either in the Old or the New Testament, endeavour to do it in a serious disposition of mind, with your heart raised to God in prayer for His help to understand and profit by what you read.

In the Bible, we read that "The fear of the Lord, that is wisdom, and to depart from evil is understanding."—*Job* xxviii. 28. Do not forget this: strive to live in the fear and love of God; that is, the fear of offending Him by doing wrong; and the love of Him, which will lead you to strive to please Him.

I will suppose that you know that you are a sinner, that you have often disobeyed the holy, just God, that you have displeased Him, and deserve His anger.

If you do know this, and are really and truly sorry for your sins, it will comfort you to think that

INTRODUCTION.

Jesus Christ, the Son of God, the Saviour of mankind, pitied us, and came into the world to save sinners; that He died on the cross for our sakes, that as by one man's (Adam's) disobedience many were made sinners, so by the obedience of one (Jesus Christ) should many be made righteous.

Think of the great love of your Heavenly Father to you—to us all—in giving us our daily bread and every comfort we enjoy; but, above all, remember His love to us in sending His beloved Son Christ Jesus into the world, to save those who believe in Him from the wrath to come; for the *wages* of sin is *death*, but the *gift* of God is eternal *life* through Jesus Christ our Lord.

Should you at any time meet with a book in which the Bible, or our blessed Saviour, are spoken of with irreverence, in a way to make people laugh, you may be sure that is a bad book; avoid it as you would a cup of poison; such books are poison to the mind.

In some families very foolish books are to be found, such as novels, plays, love stories, and such like; and sometimes foolish ballads may be brought to the door: take care not to meddle with such kind of reading, it will do you harm instead of good.

What little time you have for reading, you should endeavour to employ in such books as are improving and useful, remembering that the Bible is the best book; it is the written word of God.

Advice to Servants in general.

When girls first leave home, they often go to live where there is no fellow-servant, and this is called a place of all work.

If you are placed in such a situation, and your mistress is so kind as to teach you to do your work well, and your master and mistress are good people, who take proper care of you, and who you have reason to believe really love and fear God, then be thankful for such a place, even though your wages may be small. Do your best, and be grateful to your mistress for teaching you, and try to stay in your place. Such a situation is likely to be much better for you, till you are grown older and have had more experience, than a place where there is not only your master and mistress to please, but many fellow-servants to please also.

Try to improve as fast as you can, that you may become more useful while you stay in this place, and more fit to engage in another, when it may become proper for you to make a change.

I should hope that your master and mistress may be such as will think it right to make way for you often to go to some place appointed for the worship of Almighty God. When they give you this privilege, go there soberly; and when you are there, remember that you go to worship God and learn your duty: behave with seriousness and reverence; attend to what you hear; and when the service is over return home quickly, and try to keep your mind in a state to profit by what you have heard.

Do not, for the sake of high wages, go to any service where you are not allowed time to attend some place of worship.

Remember that God created the world in six days, and rested on the seventh, and hallowed it; therefore do not make the Sabbath a day for jaunting about, merry-making, &c.

A learned and pious man, Judge Hale, who died long ago, writes thus to his children :—" The due observance of the Sabbath, and of the duties of it, has been of singular comfort and advantage to me ; and I doubt not it will prove so to you. I have found by a strict and diligent observation, that a due observance of this day has ever had joined to it a blessing upon the rest of my time; and the week that has been so begun has been blessed and prosperous to me. And, on the other side, when I have been negligent of the duties of this day, the rest of the week has been unsuccessful and unhappy in my worldly employments ; and this I do not write inconsiderately, but from a long and sound observation and experience."

Take care what company you keep. If you see or know of any persons doing wrong things, stealing, telling lies to hide their faults, pilfering little things, talking foolishly, singing indecent songs, saying bad words, cursing, swearing, or taking God's holy name into their mouths in a vain, trifling manner, or who show a cruel disposition towards man or beast; be sure to keep out of their way. Be with them as little as you can, and talk to them as little as you may: you do not know what harm they may do you. Bad people may try to make you do wicked things that they may be able to speak ill of you; and thus keep you in fear of exposing any of *their* evil ways lest they should TELL OF YOU. But how happy are those of whom no one can tell anything that is bad!

The desire to do an act in secret, lest it may be known, should always lead you to reflect, and seriously consider whether that act is not a wrong one. "For every one that doeth evil hateth the light, neither cometh to the light, lest his deeds should be reproved. But he that doeth truth cometh to the light that his deeds may be made manifest that they are wrought in God."—*John* iii. 20, 21.

Let your dress be neat and plain, but not fine: a fine dress is very unbecoming for a servant. See 1 *Timothy* ii. 9: "I will that women adorn themselves in modest apparel, with shamefacedness and sobriety; not with broidered hair, or gold, or pearls, or costly array, but (which becometh women professing godliness) with good works."

If persons see a young woman too much dressed for her situation in life, it often gives them an ill opinion of her, and sometimes leads bad men to take improper liberties with her. Expensive dress is also improper for a servant, because it takes too much of her wages; and even supposing it should make her look like her mistress, do you think that would do her any good? I should think it far more likely to do her harm.

Be very careful never to use wicked words, nor take the name of God into your mouth without occasion. Take care never to say "God bless me!" and such like expressions, in a light and trifling manner: remember one of God's great commandments is, "Thou shalt not take the name of the Lord thy God in vain."

If you hear people cursing or swearing, go out of hearing if you can.

Be strictly honest: do not forget that you have no right to anything that belongs to your master or mistress. Do you think it would be honest to give away their bread and butter, and beer, and such like? Surely not; then remember never to do so.

Do you think it would be right to go to your mistress's cupboard, and eat the sugar and sweet things she has in it? I hope you know better.

Do you think that you have any right to take the fruit out of your master's garden? I think you know that you have not.

But if there is plenty of fruit, and your mistress gives you leave to gather some, or to pick up what has fallen off, then you may do it with pleasure.

If your clothes want mending, do you think it would be honest to take your mistress's needles and thread to work with? Surely not; so keep a little of your own.

Sometimes, most likely, you may have an accident, and break a plate or a basin, or something else; though you should be careful to break as little as you can; but if you have broken anything, always tell that you have done so; never tell a lie to hide it; and if you are really sorry for your carelessness, and take more care another time, very likely your mistress will forgive you; but even if she should be angry with you, it will be a great deal better than to have told a lie, and displeased God.

It is of great consequence to you how you behave, particularly to persons of the other sex; for there are in the world many bad men, and perhaps you may meet with some; therefore be on your guard. There are bad old men, and bad young men, both rich and poor, who are so wicked as to delight in leading young girls into wickedness and wretchedness; therefore take care how you behave to men and boys: do not be too free with them, and be sure you never laugh if you hear them say improper things, but leave them, or modestly go on with your work, without saying anything. If some people should call you proud, or such like, for not joining in their idle talk, never mind them: true humility does not consist in boldness and improper freedom; no, no, that is not the kind of humility that will lead to honour and happiness.

Be modest: modesty is the safeguard of virtue. A girl must either be bold or thoughtless, if she will strip to wash herself in the kitchen, in order to save the trouble of carrying the water up-stairs into her bed-room; for if one of the men should come in and find her undressed, and be rude to her she will be to blame as well as he. If a man begins to praise you for your beauty, or anything else, take care, do not listen or laugh, but rather leave the room.

But if any man should offer to take indecent liberties with you, tell your parents or your mistress directly; and, if needful, give warning, and leave the place as soon as you can.

Wherever you are, be on your guard against receiving complimentary notice from those who make the appearance of gentlemen, whether young or old: the gratification of vanity, in being flattered, has ruined many an unsuspecting girl.

Be prudent. Many a girl has been ruined by staying out late at night.

When you are allowed to go and see your parents and friends, be sure to return at the time fixed by your mistress. Take notice how much time it takes you to walk there, and allow as much time for walking back. Do not foolishly stop beyond the time, though your friends may wish you to stay with them. If they are true friends to you, they will not want you to get the displeasure of your mistress by staying past the right time.

If a girl stays out but one night without leave it is enough to cast a blot upon her good name, which many people will perhaps never forget, even though she may not have been doing anything wrong; people will be so apt to think that there is something not right.

Sometimes people are so foolish as to stop the clock, or hide a girl's bonnet, to keep her from going away sooner than they like: but such tricks are as unkind as they are childish.

Many girls have been ruined by the company they have met at fairs, wakes, feasts, tea-gardens, public-houses, and such like places; therefore if you value your happiness, beware how you go to such places.

Do not desire more liberty than your mistress thinks proper to give you; nor be discontented and sullen when not allowed as much as you would like: remember, your time is paid for by your food, and lodging, and your wages.

Beware of hasty promises: it is easy to say what may make you very sorry afterwards, wishing you had never said it.

Beware of passion: many persons have done things in a moment of passion, which they have bitterly repented as long as they have lived.

Did you ever see a man driving a wedge into a log of wood, to split it? He first puts the small edge into the crack, and then by driving it a little way at a time, he gets it forced in, till the thickest part is deep sunk in the wood; and what was at first only a little crack, becomes a deep, broad opening, which will soon run right through the log. Just so does the enemy of our soul's happiness contrive to get his temptations into our hearts. When he wants to make people thieves, or drunkards, or liars, or murderers, he does not at once tempt them to do a great wickedness, for he knows that they would be afraid and ashamed to do it; but he begins with some little sin, and then, when a person has done that, he is ready with a greater one, and so on, till he has got them to commit the greatest crimes, such as at first they would have trembled to think of. Therefore beware of his little temptations.

If you wish to keep him from getting in the large end of the wedge, take care that you do not let him put in the little end.

You wish to be honest; you think that you are quite sure that you never would rob your master or mistress. Very well: then never allow yourself to open their drawers, or touch their money, or clothes, except when it is your business to do so.

You think that you are in no danger of breaking the Seventh Commandment; then do not be free with young men whom you do not intend to marry, lest you come to this at last.

Do not talk to men unless they first speak to you, and then be very careful what you say. I believe very few good husbands have been met with in this way. It is a reproach for a young woman to court a man, and nothing will be more likely to make him turn away in disgust.

Never romp with great boys; it will be a blot in your character, even if you mean no harm.

But if you mean no harm, the tempter may be trying to get the little end of the wedge in; so beware, and do not play on the brink of the pit of destruction, when you ought to be walking straight on towards heaven.

Remember, that though you may commit some of these sins, without your master or mistress seeing or knowing, yet that the eye of God is ever on you, that He sees and knows all your thoughts and actions.

We read in the Bible that "all things are naked and opened unto the eyes of Him," that is God, "with whom we have to do."—*Hebrews* iv. 13.

You think it is impossible that you should ever become a drunkard; then do not take the least drop of brandy or gin. It is by taking a little and a little that most drunkards have begun.

Never take a glass of spirits, or a large draught of ale or porter, because you are tired or faint. You had better go and sit down for a quarter of an hour, and eat a bit of the hard crust of the loaf, without butter, and with a very little beer or water; you will be likely to find it give you more lasting strength.

You have, perhaps, heard of people in fevers being so strong that it took three or four people to hold them; but when the fever went away they were as weak as a child: and indeed, very often they sink away after it and die.

And it is just so with those who take spirits; they feel a little better for it at first; they think themselves stronger, and more fit for their work. But look at them in a few hours, and all their strength is gone; they want another dram, and so they go on till they become downright tipplers, and often either die in a fit, or by some inward complaint their drinking has brought on them.

Therefore keep out the little end of the wedge, the little sip of spirits.

Behave respectfully to your master and mistress. Be not saucy to them, nor pout, nor sulk, nor slam the doors, if you are not pleased; but do what they bid you quickly and cheerfully. Do not mind any little things that are disagreeable. Nobody has everything they like, so it is useless for you to expect it; but if you meet with any real hardship, speak properly to your mistress about it; tell her of it in a respectful manner, without grumbling, and perhaps she will remove the difficulty.

If there are children in the family, be kind to them, and put up with any little trouble they may give you. Remember, if you have to clean after them a good deal, that it is a part of your work, and it is not likely your mistress will expect you to do two things at once.

Take care not to talk nonsense to them; do not deceive them, nor frighten them.

If your parents are in want, give them part of your wages. Remember how much they have done for you. Have they not nursed you, and fed you, and clothed you, when you were not able to do it for yourself? Then I hope it will be a pleasure as well as a duty, to help them a little now, in return for their kindness.

But if at present they do not want your help, then as soon as you can, properly, lay by a part of your wages in the savings' bank; for should you be sick, or out of place, it will be pleasant to have something of your own. Or should you ever want to furnish a little cottage to live in, you would want money to do it with. At the savings' bank they will take as small a sum as one shilling, and keep it safe till you want it.

But if you should ever live in a profitable place, and can afford to spare a little, as well as save a little, I wish you not to grow stingy; but recommend you sometimes, when you see occasion, to give a little help to those in distress, either to your own relations or others. I think this will be doing as you would wish to be done by, supposing you were sick and in distress at home, and your sister or your acquaintance was in health, and getting high wages.

Be very careful of fire. Do not set the candles near the bed or the window curtain, nor carry them about when they want snuffing, nor set them under a shelf, nor hold them over a drawer where linen, or paper, and such things are kept; nor let the snuff fall on the shavings or the floor; use the snuffers before carrying the candles about, and do not leave them burning in the room, put them out carefully with the extinguisher at night.

Perhaps you do not know that some people are so very imprudent as to read in bed with the candle near them. If you wish not to be burnt in your bed, never do this. There are proper times for all proper things—sleeping in bed, reading and working when up.

A servant, whose carelessness has been the cause of setting a house on fire, is liable to pay a penalty of one hundred pounds, or be sent to prison for eighteen months.

Never go out without leave; and when you are sent out do not loiter by the way, but return home quickly.

Do not be idle: you are paid for your time, and by idly wasting it you may injure your master more than you think.

Endeavour to keep your clothes well mended. Keep a needle and thread ready for use, without having to seek them when wanted; and remember that "A stitch in time saves nine."

Try to be as clean as you can at all times. Wash your hands, if dirty, before you go to make up the beds; and if you live in a nice clean house, put on a clean apron also.

If you have the advantage of going early to bed at night, be sure you rise early in the morning. What mistress, do you think, would like to meet her servant just coming down stairs when much of her morning's work ought to have been done, and find no breakfast ready, no fire lighted and everything in confusion: when if she had risen early she might have had time to get through her business comfortably?

SERVANTS IN GENERAL.

Should you not have been used to rising in proper time, you will find this a fault which few mistresses can suitably overlook. The habit of early rising may be gained by those who are really desirous of it; and it is remarked that persons can, by a little perseverance, wake at the time they wish, if they strive so to do, without being called.

Should your mistress, or children, or your fellow-servant be afflicted with illness, while you are blessed with health, wait upon them cheerfully and willingly, be attentive and kind to them; for gentle and kind behaviour to the sick is very agreeable, and the contrary very unpleasant. It may be in your power to lessen the affliction of sickness by your kindness, or to add to it by your sullen, unfeeling conduct.

We none of us know how soon sickness may overtake us, when we ourselves may want the kind assistance of others.

Be moderate in your eating and drinking; eating too much is bad for your health, and drinking too much leads to misery.

I do not think it wise for young servant girls to accustom themselves to drink strong tea, with a great deal of sugar; for after awhile, should they have to buy for themselves, they will find it very expensive to do so, and if they have been accustomed to use it, they may find it hard to leave off.

A girl, little more than thirteen years old, came into the family of a friend of mine for awhile, to help the house-maid, who was much engaged in attending a sick chamber. The girl was to have her food, and sixpence per week. Her mistress found that she very much wished for a box to keep her clothes in, and told her that if she thought she could do without sugar in her tea (of which she liked a great deal) she would give six shillings to buy her a box; that if afterwards she chose sugar she might have it, but then the box was to be her mistress's; but she never began the sugar again. And some time after, her mistress told her she would give her another sixpence a week, if she liked it, instead of tea; so she left off her tea, and took milk and water with her bread and butter twice a day.

These instances of self-denial, in the beginning of a life of service, appeared to be of lasting use to her. She has now long been a respectable servant, in a family who value her highly, and has placed a nice little sum of money in the savings' bank.

Should it be a part of your business to kill chickens, or any other creatures, do not keep them too long without food before it is done; and endeavour to do it as quickly as you can, and with as little pain to the poor animal.

We read in the Bible that "Blessed are the merciful for they shall obtain mercy."

SERVANTS IN GENERAL.

If you are set to clear the house of flies or other disagreeable insects, kill them as quickly as you can; endeavour to give no unnecessary pain to the meanest creature that has life.

Should the dairy be a part of your business, and you have to milk the cows, and be much amongst the men servants, behave modestly, and do not allow any indecent jokes: take care to milk the cows quite dry, and keep everything about the dairy thoroughly clean, that the butter and cheese may be good.

When you are cooking keep a bright fire, but not larger than is wanted; and when the meat is roasting stir the fire gently lest the dust should fly about, and the cinders drop into the dripping-pan, which makes a sad smell in the house, and will most likely make the meat taste badly.

When you boil meat remember to set it on the fire in a saucepan of cold water, and let it boil slowly. Take care that no dust or soot falls into the saucepan, to prevent which keep the lower part of the chimney swept down every morning before the fire is lighted.

For boiling cabbage, or the like, take a large saucepan, that there may be room for plenty of water; let it boil up in bubbles; put in some salt, then the cabbage; keep it down with a fork a little while, then let it boil quick, with the lid off, till tender. Cabbage wants a good deal of water to make it a nice green colour, and eat well: and take care where you pour it out.

When you have potatoes to boil, put them into cold water, and boil them about twenty minutes; then pour off the water, take them out with a fork and peel them, if not done before; dry them by the fire, in the saucepan. Some potatoes will do pared raw, though some are thought best when pared after they are boiled. When this is all done, keep them in the saucepan, but without the lid, near the fire, till the rest of the dinner is ready, that they may be hot when set on the table.

A good cook likes to have all the dinner sent up nice and hot, but this wants good method and management.

When you know what is for dinner, think how long the meat should be at the fire; then consider what o'clock it should be put down, and when the pudding should be put in the pot; then get all ready and make it in good time to put in the pot at the right time, and the potatoes, &c., the same, and before the dinner is taken up consider what plates and dishes will be wanted; take them off the shelves, dust them, and put them near the fire, to be warm and at hand, with everything else that is likely to be wanted, that you may not have to run about and seek them when all should be ready, and your master and mistress's dinner be set upon the table.

A little care of this kind prevents confusion and ill-humour.

Should it be your business to put the dinner on the parlour table, lay the cloth in good time, and set the dinner on tidily; the meat at one end, and the pudding at the other; the potatoes at one side and the greens on the other; and the melted butter, or the castors in the middle.

Do not wait at table in a dirty apron, nor with dirty hands.

Wash the tea-things in hot water, but not boiling, and all glass in cold water. Put the tea-spoons in first, and rub them bright and dry; and if the bottoms of the tea-cups are become brown by the hardness of the water, it may be removed by rubbing them with a little soap. Leave the lids of the tea and coffee-pots open to prevent their getting musty, which is frequently the case if they are put by with the lid shut and not quite dry. Be careful to keep them bright and clean; if they are rubbed a little every morning it might save trouble at the end of the week.

Mind not to use boiling or hot water in washing japanned ware, as it very soon cracks or spoils.

Do not throw the brushes and flannels wet into a corner and leave them there till they smell badly, which they will do, but dry them before putting them away. Do not take the tea-cloths to clean the grates, or other dirty things; nor yet the towel to wipe the cups with; nor the knife-cloth nor pudding-cloth to rub the table; but keep all, as much as you can, for their proper uses, and in their proper places; it would be an awkward thing to have lost the pudding-cloth when the pudding ought to be boiling.

Forethought, or good contrivance, is a valuable quality, yet one in which some young persons are sadly wanting. But the peace and comfort of a family may be much promoted by it: as frequently, from the want of proper management, much confusion and quarrelling are occasioned.

By setting about the work at the wrong time, doing that first which should be last, great and uncomfortable bustle may be occasioned in the family, which by a little good management might be avoided.

If your mistress were going out after breakfast, and told you to clean the parlour, and to make some pancakes, and boil some potatoes and cabbage, to eat with the cold meat for dinner, you should first put a shovelful of coals on the kitchen fire, if wanted, to keep it from going out. Then consider what would be necessary, whether there were eggs and milk and flour in the house to make the pancakes, and whether there were the potatoes and the cabbage, and all that would be wanted, and if not, go and fetch them or send for them. Then begin to clean the parlour; after a while put more coals on the kitchen fire, and some water to heat. By this management, when cooking-time came, things would be ready at hand.

But suppose you were heedless, forgot to get the eggs and flour, and when dinner-time was nearly come, found that there was no milk in the house, that you had forgot to look at the kitchen-fire so that was gone out; that there was no wood ready to light it with, but you must go into the yard, and chop some up; run one way to the shop for eggs, and another way for the milk and the flour; and then, when the dinner ought to be on the table, find no hot water for the cabbage; the fire would not burn; you could not get the pancakes ready, the potatoes almost raw, no time to lay the cloth, and all in confusion; you would find, that though you had cleaned the parlour nicely, you had not managed well, because you had not done things at the proper time, when, with a little good contrivance, all might have been done comfortably, to your mistress's satisfaction, and your own credit.

A careless servant, who manages thus badly, or who spoils the butter for want of cleanliness in the dairy; or who, when cooking, over-roasts the meat, or else sends it to table almost raw; who burns the bread and the pies, when baking them; who spoils the potatoes, and sends up the greens not fit to be eaten; who keeps herself either so dirty or so fine as not to be fit to be seen, cannot expect to stay in her place, to be as much respected, and receive as much wages, as the young woman who behaves well, and tries to do everything to the satisfaction of her master and mistress.

If you wish to become a valuable servant, learn also to be frugal; and if you get such a habit while you are young, it may prove of great service to you as you grow older, and have to manage for yourself.

If you often think of the old saying, "Waste not, want not," it may be of use to you, as waste often leads to want. Besides, do you think it would be right to waste your master's property, when, with a little care, you might avoid it?

A master may lose a great deal by a careless servant. There are many ways of wasting. Suppose you let two or three candles stand burning in the kitchen, when one is enough, that is waste; and so it is to keep a great fire burning when only a small one is wanted. Coals, in many places, cost a great deal of money, and should be used carefully, and so should the bread: bread is sometimes called the staff of life, because we should not know what to do without it; and the bits should be eaten soon after being cut off, when they are fresh and good, and not kept till they are unfit to eat, and then thrown into the hog-tub; but if by chance too much has been cut at one meal, cover it up, and bring it out to be eaten at the next.

SERVANTS IN GENERAL.

Take care not to leave the soap in the water to melt away and come to nothing, but when not in use keep it dry.

If you have the care of silver spoons, count them very often to see that they are right: and if, at any time, one should be missing, tell your mistress directly. Do not suppose that it may be here, or it may be there, and so let it be quite lost without her knowledge; do not leave them lying about, but take care to keep them in their proper place.

Remember, too, that cups and saucers, plates and dishes, wine-glasses and window panes are very expensive, and will be easily broken if you handle them roughly; and your carelessness may cost your master a deal of money, and bring you into trouble too.

But when you try to do your best, and your mistress sees that you wish to do right, and to please her, then it is likely things will go on well and comfortably.

Yet wherever we live, and whether we are poor or rich, we must not expect that everything will go on just as we should like; for every one meets with some things that are disagreeable.

If you have the care of a wash, wash the linen thoroughly, rinse, and boil it well; then make it a nice colour, neither too blue nor yellow. Some things want a great deal more blue than others.

Then iron or mangle it nicely and dry it well. Flannel does best in hot water, with but little soap. Remember, if you put damp linen with that which is dry, the dry will become damp also. If you have the care of linen which has been put out to wash, dry it well when it comes home; but lest it should have got a little dampness afterwards, put the sheets, &c., to the fire again, before they are put on the beds. If you have the care of beds, let the spare ones, in winter time especially, be slept in two or three nights, or otherwise aired every fortnight. Damp beds are very dangerous.

When rain comes down the chimneys look at the grates and wipe it off them, if they are bright, lest they get rusty.

Servants ought to know whether their mistress allows any perquisites, or not; because, if a mistress agrees that her cook is to have the kitchen-stuff for her own profit, she may take it without fear; but even then she has no right to put in the ends of the candles, or the fat, or the suet, which ought to be used in the house, nor any thing else, which she thinks her mistress would not like.

But if the mistress does not allow the kitchen-stuff to her servant, then she has no right to it, and it would be dishonest to take it.

Some mistresses, in case of illness in the house, allow the servant who nurses to have the phials that are done with, for her own; but before you take or sell one, be sure that it is allowed, or you will be taking that which belongs to your master or mistress.

You never need to be at a loss to know what is stealing, and what is not, if you will only think of one thing, or ask yourself one question—Should I take this if master was by? If your conscience tells you no, you may be sure it would be stealing; and remember God sees everything; He is everywhere.

Shop-Maid.

If you wish to be employed in a shop when you leave school, you should endeavour to improve as much as possible while there, particularly in needle-work, writing, and accounts; for you need not expect that any person, qualified to manage a business properly, would choose to engage an assistant in the shop who could not reckon readily, make out bills properly, and add them up correctly; and this often must be done in haste, and sometimes whilst persons are talking.

Probably you would have needle-work to do, which ought to be done quickly and well.

But as it is not easy to get a place in a shop, I would not advise you to set your mind upon it, unless there is some particular reason for thinking of the employment. But if you do gain such a situation, remember that a shop-maid should be very careful to keep the shop in order; not to let the goods lie about on the counter, lest they should be soiled or stolen: but when done with, put them neatly away in their proper places.

A shop-maid should be careful not to take bad money; but if you have taken any, never attempt to impose it on any one. You should give full weight and measure; but be exact in so doing, otherwise you may give away more than your master's profits.

You should give no credit in your master or mistress's absence, except to such as you believe they would approve; then put it down, and tell them as soon as they come home, never trusting to your memory about it.

If you are placed in a shop, there will be a great deal for you to learn, which I cannot attempt to tell you about, but which, if you wish to be clever in your business, you may feel much obliged to those who take the trouble of teaching you.

But I *can* tell you to be attentive and obliging to the customers: serve them quickly, and answer all proper questions in a civil manner; but do not waste your own time, nor induce them to spend theirs, in a great deal of trifling and unnecessary chit-chat.

Most likely you will be expected to fill up your spare time in house-work, or needle-work: if you are, be industrious in what is required of you.

Nursery-Maid.

If you are entrusted with the care of children, you should consider it a very important charge. Your conduct and behaviour may have a very great influence on the character of the dear children under your care: therefore let the bent of your mind be to do them good by example, as well as by words. Pray to your Heavenly Father to enable you to discharge your duties towards them.

Take care always to speak the truth on every occasion.

Never use deceit to dry up their tears, or endeavour to please them when fretting, by saying you will take them to some place to which you never intend to go, or promise them cakes or sweets which you do not mean to give them.

Children soon discover these falsehoods, and are not likely to love those who thus deceive and disappoint them; but, above all, it is doing wrong, and teaching them to do wrong also.

Children should never be terrified by shutting them up in a dark room, or by telling them frightful stories, particularly about ghosts, and such like, with which some foolish people cruelly impose on the fears of poor little children.

Never do or say any such things to them; but if you find them hard to manage, tell your mistress about it in a proper manner, without passion or grumbling, and if she knows that you are kind to them, perhaps she will help you about it.

I have read a very sad story of a silly nursery-maid, which is only one out of many that might be told.

A little girl, about six years old, whose mother was going out visiting, was permitted to be in the room whilst she was dressing. There happened to be some fine things left about after she was gone, and the child amused herself by playing with them, and while doing so she threw down a looking-glass and broke it to pieces. The maid, coming in and seeing what was done, was displeased, and instead of talking to her, and blaming her gently, she thought she would frighten the poor little girl; so she made herself a very odd figure, and went into the room again, and spoke to her in a very strange and unkind manner. But the silly woman had great reason to repent of what she had done; for the poor child was so terribly frightened that she fell into violent fits, and lost her senses: from which she never recovered, but became a poor little idiot.

Oh! what a sad thing this was, and how the poor little girl's parents must have been grieved, and how sad the nursery-maid, who had done the foolish thing, must have felt! If she had taken care of this poor little child, ever afterwards, as long as she lived, night and day, without wages, she could never make up for the mischief she had done. Let me entreat you never to attempt to manage children in any such manner; there are better ways of keeping them in order, much more likely to gain their love, and if they should be disposed to be a little wilful sometimes, they will most likely sooner do as you wish if they see you are sorry, rather than angry.

Do not encourage children, even little children, in crying for what they want; rather kindly try to amuse them with something else.

When out of your mistress's sight, neither do anything, nor say anything to them, which you would not choose she should know.

Never say anything before a child which you would not like it to say again in the parlour. Never say to a child, "You must not tell;" but if you would talk about anything you do not wish to have repeated, speak of it when the children are not with you.

Little children are sometimes fretful and peevish. Poor little creatures! they cannot tell what is the matter; so try to be very patient with them. By speaking kindly and gently to them, you will be likely to gain their love, and make them and yourselves the more happy.

But in order to please a child, never suffer it to torment any living thing. Young children do not understand the pain they give to little animals they are thoughtlessly suffered to handle: the fly buzzing in the window often escapes from their fingers with its fine gauze wings quite broken off, and with the loss of some of its slender legs; whilst other poor animals often suffer from the thoughtlessness of badly-taught children.

When children have been sobbing or crying, it is very wrong to threaten them with punishment if they do not "give over directly," for they cannot help sobbing after their anger is past.

Do not encourage a child to hide any fault done either by the child, by yourself, or by any others; this is teaching it to deceive, and is a hurt to the child's mind which it is not is your power to remove.

Some children have naturally a much pleasanter temper than others, but it is not always that they are the most deserving of encouragement; for if a child with a temper naturally sullen or passionate is striving to overcome it, while the good-tempered child may be indulging itself in vanity, or pride, or other bad ways, I think you will see that the child naturally ill-tempered will most deserve your love.

And if one of the children is quick and clever, and another dull, it may happen sometimes that the dull child is taking more pains to learn his lesson, and improve, than the other, and yet cannot get on so fast.

Be gentle and kind to all the children, and try to teach them to be kind to each other; but do not expect them always to give up their playthings to the little one, who very likely would spoil them, and vex the child to whom they belong; rather, in general, let each play with their own toys, except when they incline to let each other have them.

It tries the temper of the elder children to have their little treasures spoiled; and the little ones should not be indulged in having everything they see.

Endeavour to keep yourselves, as well as the children, clean; but try not to encourage a love of finery in them. Do not admire their dress when they are in the room, nor speak of their pretty new shoes, nice frock, &c. I think it best not to talk to them about fashions, but teach them to keep their clothes clean, and not to tear them.

Be particularly careful not to let the children play at an open window, and do not leave them in a room with a fire or candle within their reach: many poor children have been burned to death by getting too near the fire.

In walking out with the children, go no farther than your mistress allows, nor to any place she wishes you to keep away from; do not stay out longer than she approves, nor yet keep the poor little things running by your side faster than their little short legs can properly carry them, to make up for the time you have sauntered away.

Children often suffer from young nursery-maids being induced thoughtlessly to stop and talk with their acquaintance in the cold, instead of walking on and minding their business; but this is not the way to please a good mistress.

Do not tease the children, but rather comfort them in their little troubles. For instance, if a child is shy, do not talk of sending him away with a stranger who may happen to speak to him, but rather let him see that you are going to keep him with you. I believe the shyness of children sometimes arises from the fear of strangers, and that in this they want a little kind consideration.

Never indulge a child in what his mother has forbidden, for that would be disobeying your mistress, and teaching him also to be disobedient to his mother.

In short, endeavour to act with justice and kindness toward the children, and set them a good example; and may you be blessed in your endeavour for their good, and feel the sweet reward of peace in your own mind.

Advice to Servants about to change their Places.

When it is *necessary* for you to change your place, take care where you offer your service.

But if you are in a comfortable and safe situation, be very careful to let no trifling inconveniences unsettle you.

There are many situations in which even a steady and virtuous young woman is in great danger of losing her character. This should make you very particular in knowing that you are likely to engage with persons of correct conduct.

This danger exists in the country as well as in town; but what makes it greater in towns is, that there it is not so easy to learn the character of families.

Some persons have been so hasty and inconsiderate as to turn a girl out of doors if she has displeased them, without giving her time to get into a proper lodging. This, if she has not behaved very badly, is a sad case, and if she is in a strange place, she may be dreadfully exposed, so as to lose her health before she gets home or obtains another place; or, what is far worse, she may be taken in to lodge by one of those wicked wretches, who pretend to show kindness to friendless girls only that they may make them as wicked as themselves, and ruin them for this world as well as the next.

But as you would no doubt be sorry that anything so distressing should happen to you, I would earnestly advise you to get your mother, your schoolmistress, or some prudent woman, to inquire for you before you engage in a place:—

1. Whether the family bears a good character?

2. Whether they go to any place of worship? and if so, whether they will allow you to go to one at least once in the week?—for if you have not this privilege, very likely you will become unmindful of your religious duties, and careless of your conduct.

Places where high wages are given are not always the best.

In choosing an adviser, do not go to those who flatter you, but rather choose such as would be honest and kind enough to tell you if they saw the fault was your own instead of your master's or mistress's, when you thought of changing your place.

Flatterers generally have their own ends in view, it is not often out of any kindness to you that they talk so smoothly: while those who wish well to us are more likely to tell us of our faults than to feed our vanity by praising us.

If you live in the fear of God, behave well, and take care where you go to live you are not likely to be ill-treated by anyone; but if you should ever have reason to believe that your character is in danger from any of the family you live with, lose no time before you consult your parents, or such of your female friends as you look up to.

I do not mean to advise you to be telling every little thing you do not like in your place: this would be imprudent, and perhaps give you the character of a "tell-tale." Besides, you should not forget, that wherever you go you will find some things you do not like.

A girl of good character from the country, whose master and mistress are dead, or who has in any manner lost her home in London, or other large place, should think directly, before she has spent all her money, whether it is not best for her to return to her relations, lest she should fall into bad company at unawares and be ruined.

After a few years, very likely some of you may have proposals of marriage, but if you value your own happiness, be very careful how you listen to what is said to you on the subject; do not think that every man who takes notice of you intends or wishes to make you his wife. Remember it is a very serious thing to be bound for life; do not listen to anyone until he makes real proposals of marriage to you; nor, if you love God yourself, even then, unless you have reason to believe he really loves and fears God also; who is industrious and sober, chaste and honest, and who is likely to strengthen your own good desires after holiness; but you must judge more from his conduct than from his words. Some men will say many fine things which they do not mean; and many young women are led astray by their wicked deceit.

But if anything of this kind is named to you, or you have good reason to believe is intended by anyone, be sure you take the first opportunity to tell your best friends about it, and ask their advice.

Remember, too, that marrying very young, before you have gained experience, got a good stock of strong, useful clothes, and saved some money against a rainy day, will be very likely to lead you into wretched poverty.

But if you have lived long enough single to have gained experience, and a good character, and saved money enough to help you in case of trouble, and then marry a truly pious man, one who, being really a Christian, is conscientiously endeavouring to perform all his duties to the glory of God, and who has also saved some money to furnish your cottage, then, with His blessing, you have a comfortable prospect before you.

Most likely it will be the proper allotment of some of you to lead a single life; in which case perhaps you may have much less care; and if you perform your various duties, you may become quite as useful, and quite as respectable, as if married.

Extract from the Memoirs of Mrs. Huntingdon (p. 177).

"I called in by accident, as we say, to-day, at a miserable looking house, where I found a poor afflicted woman, of twenty or twenty-three years of age whose case affected me much. She has one child eighteen months old, and one three months old; is in miserable health herself, and has an intemperate unkind husband. She appeared broken hearted, and almost bereft of reason. She was born at———, attended Mr. ———'s ministry, and was once the subject of serious impressions; but an imprudent marriage has ruined her, at least for this world. She is in a wretched dirty hovel with her husband, father, and mother, and a flock of miserable children. All of them are addicted to drink; quarrels among parents and children, till midnight, are frequent. I saw only the mother-in-law, but the scene I witnessed was an emblem of hell. The poor young woman is in a state little short of despair. She says it is impossible for her to have a moment alone, and that her husband and mother-in law will not let her read the Bible. She said to me, 'Oh, if I could go up, and stay at your house but one night.'"

See the effects of being unhappily married to a drinking man!

Conclusion.

Before laying aside this little book, in which I hope you may have found many friendly hints, likely to be of use to you now whilst you are young, and some others to be remembered when you grow older; let me ask you not to forget that, whether single or married, rich or poor, mistress or servant, it is the blessing of the Almighty that makes truly rich; and that, without an interest in His mercy, through Jesus Christ, you could not be happy, even though you had all the riches your heart could wish, and all the pleasure you could desire.

I will now point your attention to a few texts in the new Testament, addressed to servants, which I commend to your special attention.

"Servants, be obedient to those that are your masters according to the flesh, with fear and trembling, in singleness of heart as unto Christ; not with eye-service as men-pleasers, but as the servants of Christ, doing the will of God from the heart."

CONCLUSION. 43

"With good will doing service as to the Lord and not unto men, knowing that whatsoever good thing any man doeth, the same shall he receive, whether he be bond or free."—*Ephesians* vi. 5-8.

"Servants, obey in all things your masters according to the flesh, not with eye-service as men-pleasers, but in singleness of heart, fearing God. And whatsoever ye do, do it heartily as to the Lord, and not unto men, knowing that of the Lord ye shall receive the reward of the inheritance, for ye serve the Lord Christ; but he that doeth wrong shall receive for the wrong which he hath done; and there is no respect of persons."—*Colossians* iii. 22-25.

"Exhort servants to be obedient to their own masters, and to please them well in all things, not answering again; not purloining, but showing all good fidelity; that they may adorn the doctrine of God our Saviour in all things."—*Titus* ii. 9, 10.

"Servants, be subject to your masters with all fear, not only to the good and gentle, but also to the froward. For this is thankworthy, if a man for conscience toward God endure grief, suffering wrongfully. For what glory is it, if, when ye be buffeted for your faults, ye take it patiently? but if when ye do well, and suffer for it, ye take it patiently, this is acceptable with God. For even hereunto were ye called, because Christ also hath suffered for us, leaving us an example, that ye should follow His steps, who did no sin, neither was guile found in His mouth ; who when He was reviled, reviled not again, when He suffered He threatened not, but committed Himself to Him that judgeth righteously."—1 *Peter* ii. 18-23.

Remember this text of Scripture for your encouragement in doing right: "Seek ye first the kingdom of God and His righteousness, and and all these things shall be added unto you ;" that is, all things your Heavenly Father sees needful for you.

The Request.

Father, whate'er of earthly bliss
   Thy sovereign will denies,
Accepted at Thy throne of grace
   Let this petition rise—

"Give me a calm, a thankful heart,
   From every murmur free,
The blessings of Thy grace impart,
   And make me live to Thee.

"Let the sweet hope that Thou art mine
   My life and death attend,
Thy presence through my journey shine,
   And crown my journey's end."

                                  STEELE.

Printed by Libri Plureos GmbH in Hamburg, Germany